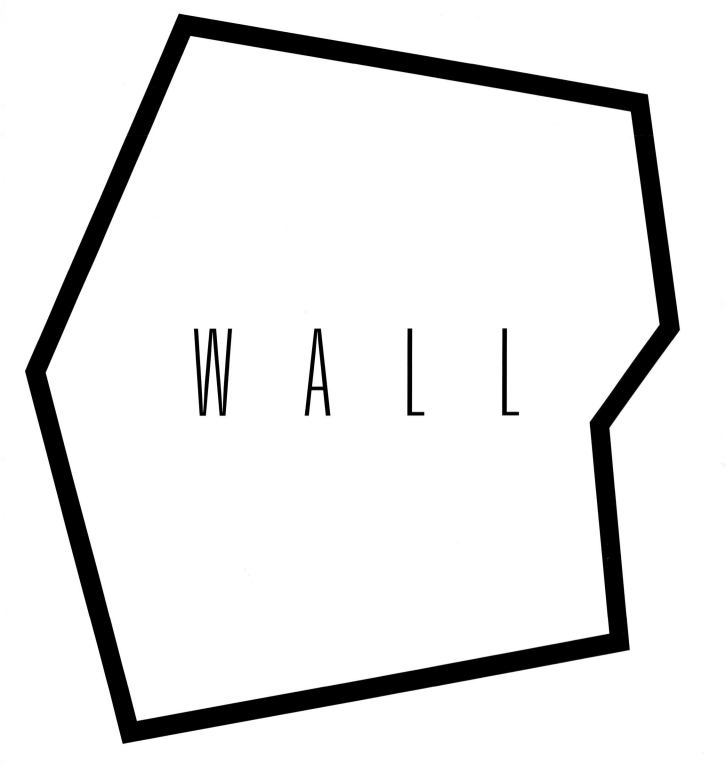

photographs by ANTOINE BOOTZ

First published in the United States
of America in 2011 by

New York, New York

Glitterati Incorporated
225 Central Park West, Suite 305
New York, New York 10024

www.GlitteratiIncorporated.com
Telephone: 212 362 9119
media@glitteratiincorporated.com for inquiries
Follow us on Facebook and Twitter
at Glitterati Buzz

First edition, 2011

Creative Director: Ken Smart
Design: Sarah Morgan Karp
In House Layout Coordinator: Zach Smart

Library of Congress Cataloging-in-Publication data
is available from the publisher.

Hardcover edition ISBN 13:
978-0-9823799-8-1

Printed and bound in China.
10 9 8 7 6 5 4 3 2 1

WALL

RALPHPUCCI

Foreword by Wendy Goodman

Glitterati
INCORPORATED

New York, New York

TO

O ANN

RALPH

ACKNOWLEDGMENTS

SOL LEWITT
JOAN MIRO
ANTONI TAPIES
PIET MONDRIAN
HENRI MATISSE
CY TWOMBLY
KEITH HARING
JEAN DUBUFFET
PABLO PICASSO
LUIS BARRAGAN
MARK ROTHKO
AGNES MARTIN
ROBERT MOTHERWELL
KENNY SCHARF
ROBERT WILSON
DAN FLAVIN
JEAN-MICHEL BASQUIAT

AARON SISKIND
DONALD JUDD
ROBERT RYMAN
ANDY WARHOL
RICHARD SERRA
ELLSWORTH KELLY
AD REINHARDT
ROBERT SMITHSON
RALPH HUMPHREY
HELEN LUNDEBERG
JOHN CHAMBERLAIN
LORSER FEITELSON
KARL BENJAMIN
RAY EAMES
JOHN McLAUGHLIN
BRICE MARDEN
ISAMU NOGUCHI

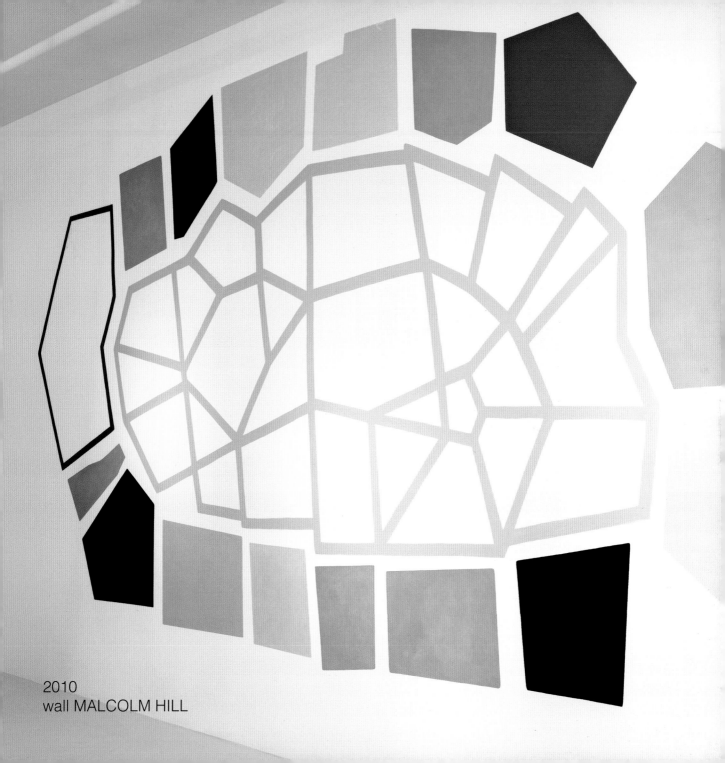

2010
wall MALCOLM HILL

2006
wall SIRICHAI

CONTENTS

2008
furniture & wall INDIA MAHDAVI

OREWORD

I am inspired every time I visit the Ralph Pucci showroom. It always starts with The Wall. This is the first thing you see when you enter the gallery. The Wall has been designated as a revolving artist's canvas complementing the featured designer's work on exhibition. It illustrates the synergy between art and design, and if it seems that each new installation of The Wall is better than the last, that is only because each one resonates so perfectly with what is displayed in front of it.

The Wall has become so much more than a space for temporary murals; it is the meeting place for artists who work in different media. This is the genius of Ralph Pucci's vision: He has always known how to challenge artists to come up with something new and exciting. He has been doing this ever since the day he joined his family's mannequin business and began exploring the creation of new models that instigated a sea change in the way we perceive fashion retail display and museum costume exhibits.

The Wall also signifies the creativity of Ralph Pucci International and how Ralph over the years has created a stable of legendary design stars while at the same time discovering new talent. Deborah Turbeville's black-and-white photographs of "The Hidden Versailles" infused The Wall with enchantment, bringing you deep into the mysteries of history; while Malcolm Hill's bold abstract painting created a stately modern background for Jim Zivic's brilliant take on coal, the most humble of earth-born materials, which he transformed into striking monuments by force of polishing their natural shapes. Patrick Naggar's furniture seemed to have been caught somewhere between earth and sky when he painted The Wall the most shimmering blue; while Andree Putman decreed that a Pompeian-painted Wall should be the visual welcome for her curve of an elegant sofa.

Diego Uchitel created a quiet oasis by placing just one photograph on The Wall as backdrop to Spencer Fung's rigorous, geometric table and chairs, pared with Chris Lehreche's poetic wood stools. The Wall became a fragment from an exquisite imaginary lost castle when it was painted the palest leaf-green with Herve Van Der Straeten's framed circular mirror hanging on it. And Ruben Toledo always invigorates The Wall in his visits to it, with his symphony of characters that live in worlds of grace and humor infused with witty chic.

In the end, The Wall becomes a transcendent element, always creating the perfect setting to introduce you into Ralph Pucci's fantastic world.

WENDY GOODMAN
New York City

2008
mirror
PHILIPPE HIQUILY

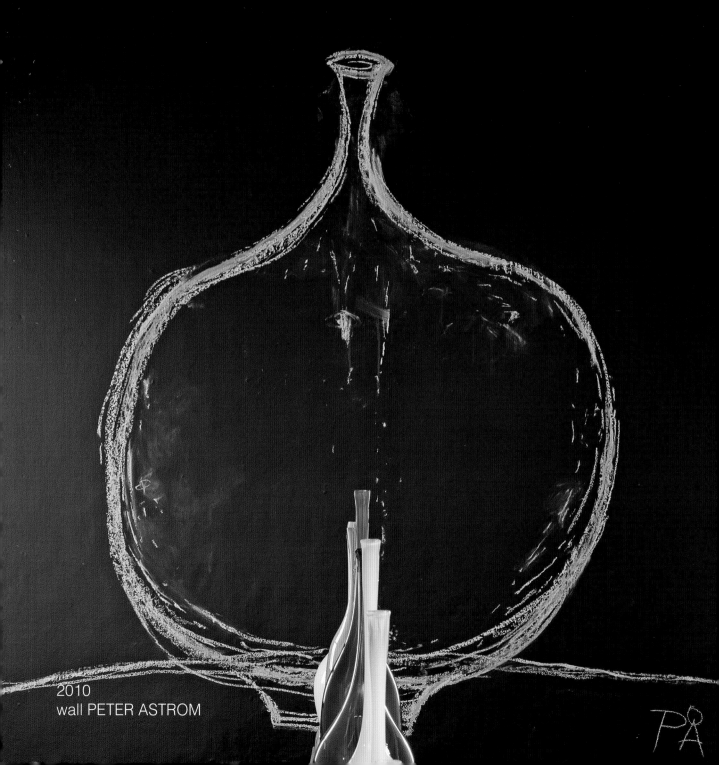

2010
wall PETER ASTROM

N T R O D U C T I O N

Over the past 20 years I have commissioned scores of amazing artists, illustrators and architects to paint the entrance wall in my NY gallery/showroom. When the exhibition ends, usually three months after the artwork is created, we repaint The Wall, creating a fresh new canvas. The concept is that each show will be another artist's opportunity to create something unique and magical. Many of my clients have suggested having the work painted on a canvas so it could be sold as an individual artwork. Instinctively, I always felt that this approach would restrict the artist's freedom in what would be created on The Wall. Precisely because the piece was temporary, and definitely not for sale, artists would be willing to take risks they might not otherwise take. I didn't want an artist to decide that a 14-by-16-foot piece might be too difficult to sell and let that limitation lead him or her to create a less substantial piece. There are other locations in the showroom for intimate pieces; but The Wall is the special, unfettered space. Nor did I want the artist encumbered with the need to take a more commercial approach to the artwork. When painting directly on The Wall there would be no inhibitions. I want a situation that creates spontaneity and improvisation, with total freedom to explore and be inspired by the artworks, usually 3-D, that may be featured in front of The Wall.

The Wall is not smooth and perfect. It is covered with imperfections, bumps, and crevasses. It creates depth and texture. It is imbued with a sense that it is permanent, it has been there, forever. Rather than The Wall itself, it is the treatment of The Wall that is ever-changing. As each artist creates his piece on a blank surface, all of the creation that has gone before him or her remains spiritually, if not actually; building layer upon layer like an ancient city that has yet to be excavated.

The purpose of this book is to demonstrate how a wall can morph into a dynamic focal area: How it sets the mood, the tone and magic of a "show." A wall can grab you and pull you into this mysterious landscape. How it creates a "wow!"

Whenever we are developing and creating a new collection to present, whether furniture, mannequins, sculpture, or art, I always envision the possibilities for The Wall. It could be simply the use of a single color–bright red to shout sexiness; or a muted gray to whisper sophistication. A mural by Ruben Toledo or Kenny Scharf will create a surrealistic pop "soundtrack." Repetition of a photograph or sculpture exudes power and strength. The use of one object on a The Wall creates the opposite effect--a zen-like calm.

There are no rules or formulas as to how The Wall can or will be treated. I frequently visit museums and galleries looking for new inspiration. My artistic heroes like Sol Lewitt, Joan Miro, and Cy Twombly have all influenced my collections and what has been transformed on The Wall. My travels have been a source of inspiration, too. The patina on a 1000-year-old Roman wall with various colors and stains from the wind, rain and sun; the starkness of graffiti on the streets of Berlin; a jazz club; a film: Any one of these can be the impetus for a specific treatment on The Wall.

Inspiration can come from almost anywhere and sometimes when you least expect it. Treating each artwork on The Wall as an art instillation has been exhilarating. When planning a new showroom, our (nine) gallery, we made certain to include a new opportunity to have The Wall 2. We now have more options to explore, to work with creative minds, and to create more "wow!"

I may have painted over all our great instillations on The Wall in the past, it's true. That has always been a part of the spirit of the space. The Wall is temporary, like a flower in bloom. I like it better this way. Each project brought to The Wall may have only lived a short life, but the mystery and excitement it has created will live forever due to the incredible Antoine Bootz, who through his photography seen here has captured the magic for all of us to savor.

Now, if walls could talk…

RALPH PUCCI
New York City

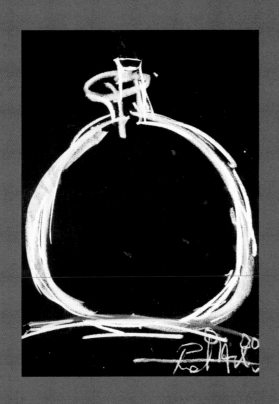

2010
art PETER ASTROM

2010
wall TOM H JOHN

2010
wall TOM H JOHN
furniture RALPH PUCCI (ONE)

2009
wall DEBORAH TURBEVILLE

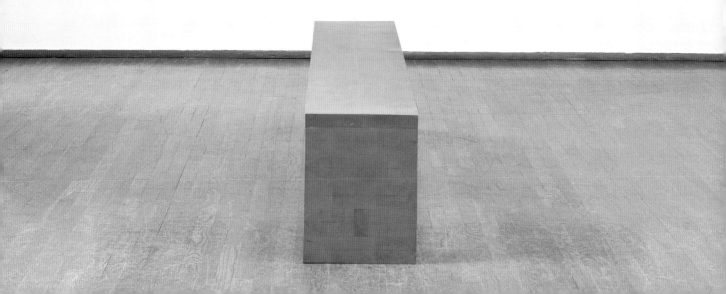

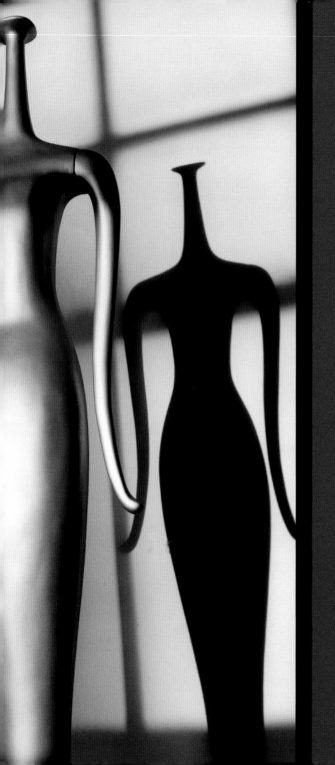

1995/2011
wall & sculpture PATRICK NAGGAR

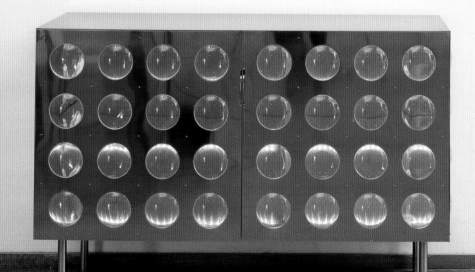

2011
wall & furniture PATRICK NAGGAR

2011
wall & furniture PATRICK NAGGAR

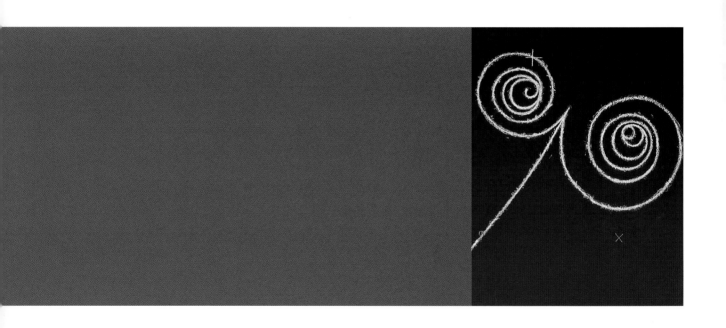

2008
wall & furniture PATRICK NAGGAR

2011
wall & furniture PATRICK NAGGAR

2004
wall & lamp PATRICK NAGGAR

2001
wall & furniture PATRICK NAGGAR

2000
wall & furniture ANDREE PUTMAN

2003
wall & furniture CHRIS LEHRECKE

2004
wall & furniture VLADIMIR KAGAN

2005
wall MALCOLM HILL
furniture JENS RISOM

2001
wall JOHN WIGMORE
mannequin BLANK

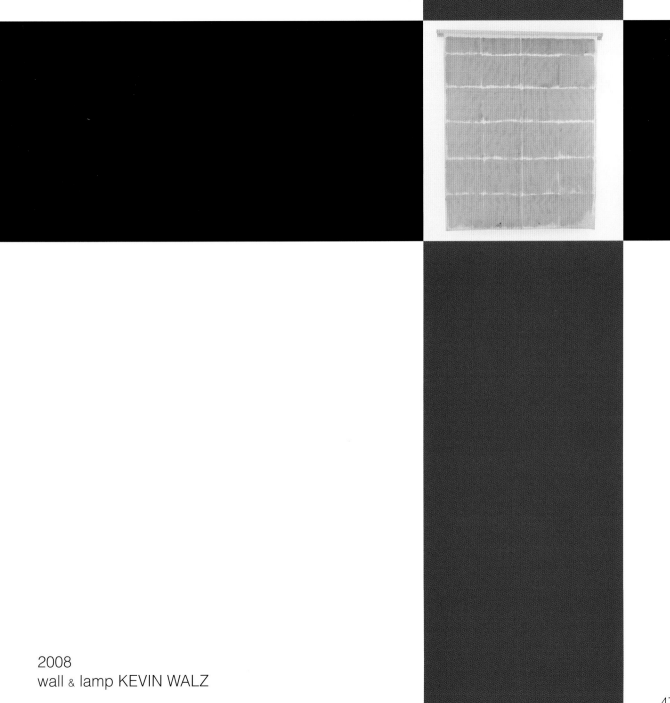

2008
wall & lamp KEVIN WALZ

DAVID WEEKS
lighting

CUS LEATHERDALE
photography

2011
wall MARCUS LEATHERDALE
furniture RALPH PUCCI (ONE)

1999
wall DIEGO UCHITEL
furniture SPENCER FUNG
pedestal CHRIS LEHRECKE

2009
wall LISA SPINDLER &
STEVI MICHNER
furniture VLADIMIR KAGAN

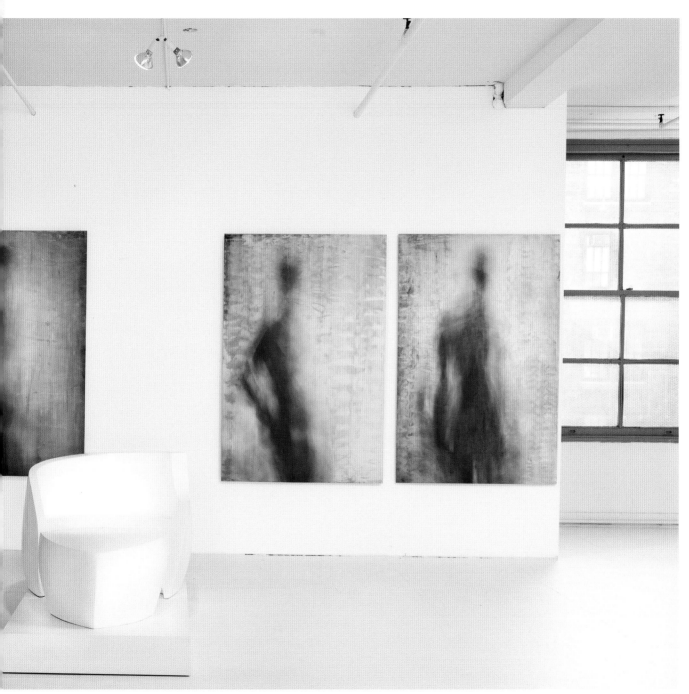

2009
wall & furniture VLADIMIR KAGAN

MANUEL GEERINCK

INSTALLATION
7–7–09

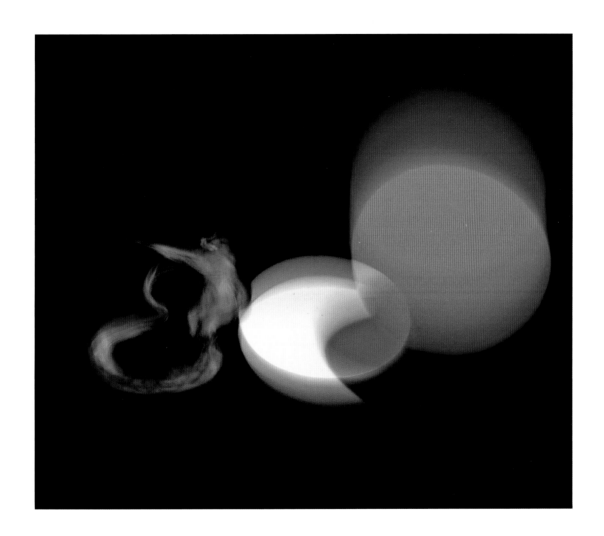

2009
wall PETER ASTROM
chair WILLIAM EMMERSON

2011
ASTROM

2010
wall PETER ASTROM

2010
wall PETER ASTROM
glass vessels LIANNE GOLD & ANDREW THOMPSON

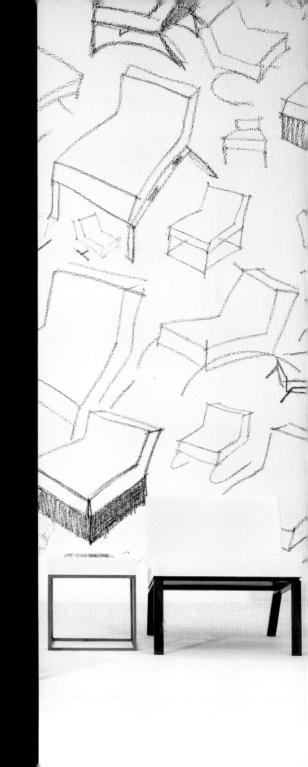

2006
wall & furniture ROBERT BRISTOW

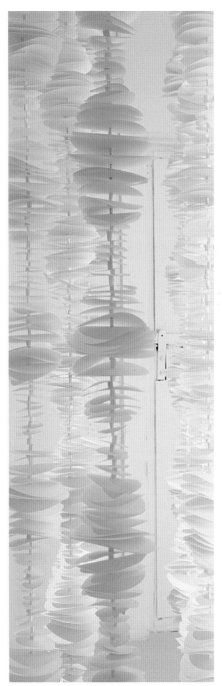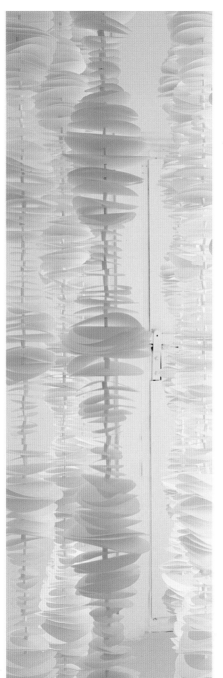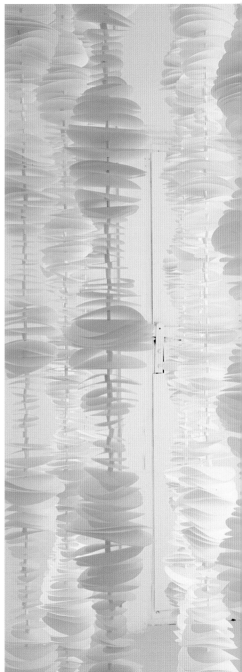

2010
wall EMILY VISLOCKY

2011
wall & fashion KC WEAKLEY

2007
wall HERVE VAN DER STRAETEN

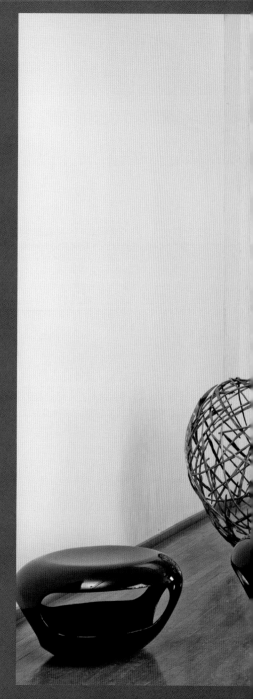

2007
wall & furniture HERVE VAN DER STRAETEN

2007
mirror HERVE VAN DER STRAETEN

JEROME ABEL SEGUIN

"LA NATURE FAIT OEUVRE D'ARTISTE"

2002
wall JEROME ABEL SEGUIN

2000
wall JEROME ABEL SEGUIN

2006
wall & furniture PAUL MATHIEU

2005
wall & sculpture JONATHAN KLINE

2009
art RUBEN TOLEDO

2000
wall & mannequins RUBEN TOLEDO

1995
wall & mannequins RUBEN TOLEDO

1993
sculpture & mannequins RUBEN TOLEDO

2005
wall ROBERTO DUTESCO
bench JEROME ABEL SEGUIN

2001
wall NICHOLAS HOWEY
mannequins BLANK

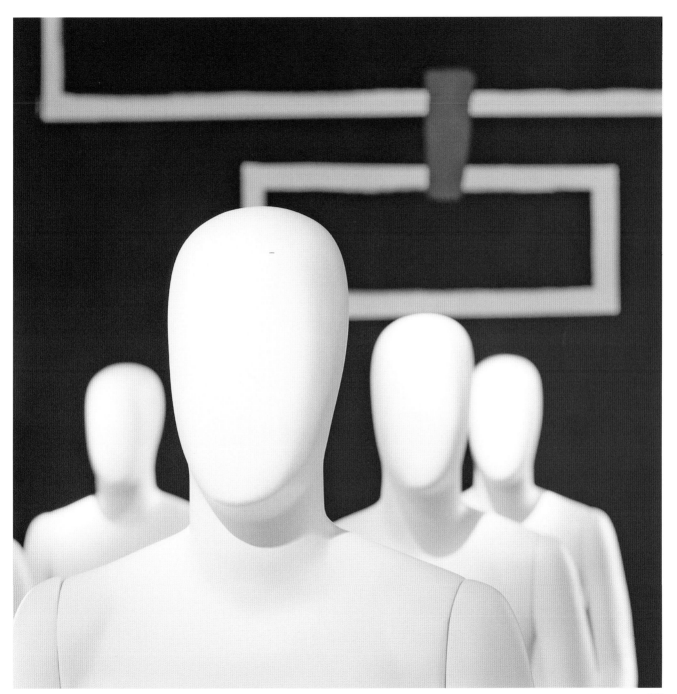

2002
wall & mannequins CHRISTY TURLINGTON

1996
wall JEFFREY FULVIMARI

2005
wall JEFF QUINN
coal JIM ZIVIC

2007
wall & furniture VICENTE WOLF

2007
wall CHRISTOPHER MAKOS

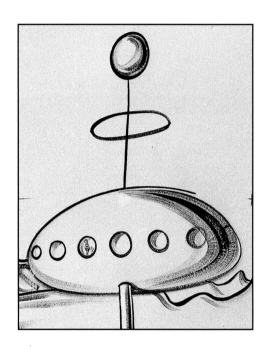

1996
wall KENNY SCHARF

1998
wall & mannequins KENNY SCHARF

1993
wall & mannequins MICHAEL BARTALOS

1994
wall & mannequins MAIRA KALMAN

2000
wall & mannequins LAURA LJUNGKVIST

1998
wall & mannequins CHESLEY McLAREN

2005
wall & mannequins ANJA KROENCKE

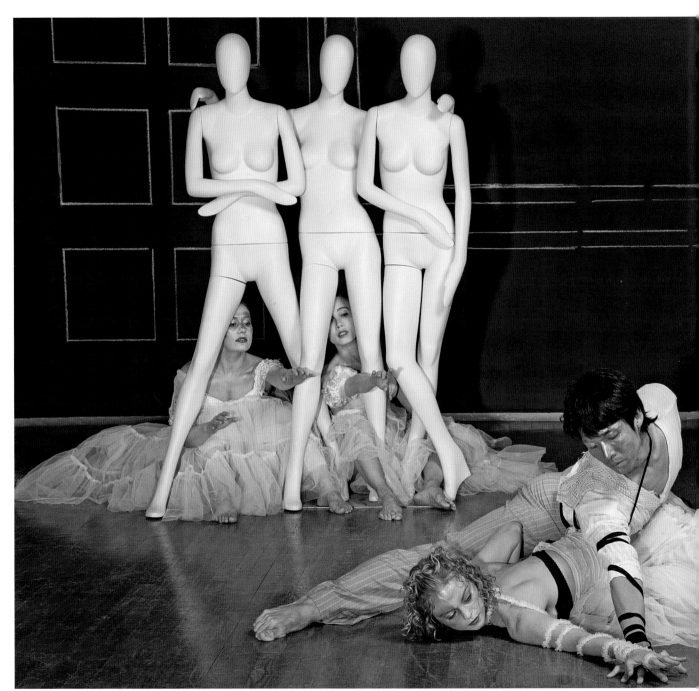

2008
wall INDIA MAHDAVI
dancers BUGLISI DANCE THEATRE
mannequin GIRL
photography © KRISTIN LODEN LINDER

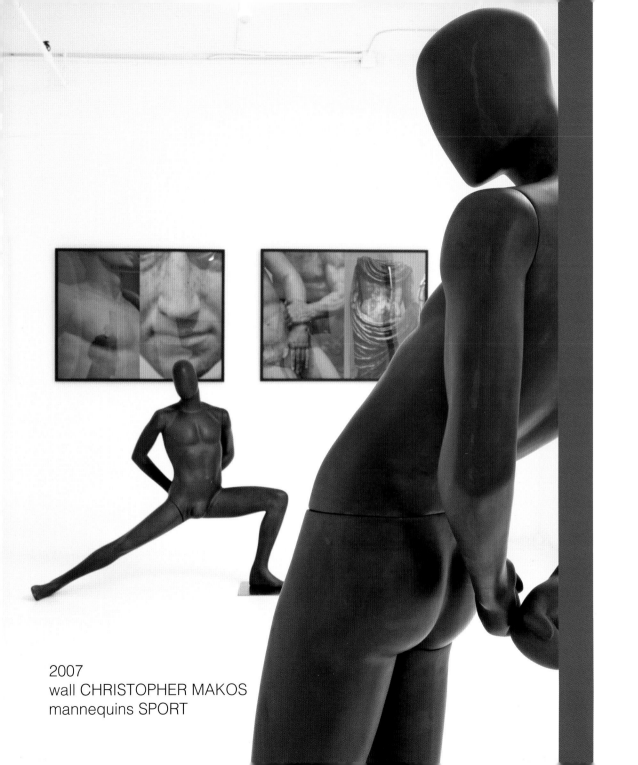

2007
wall CHRISTOPHER MAKOS
mannequins SPORT

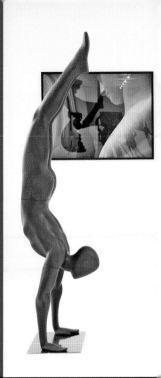

ATELIER
ERIC SCHMITT April 2011

2011
wall & furniture ERIC SCHMITT

2011
wall DANA BARNES
furniture KEVIN WALZ

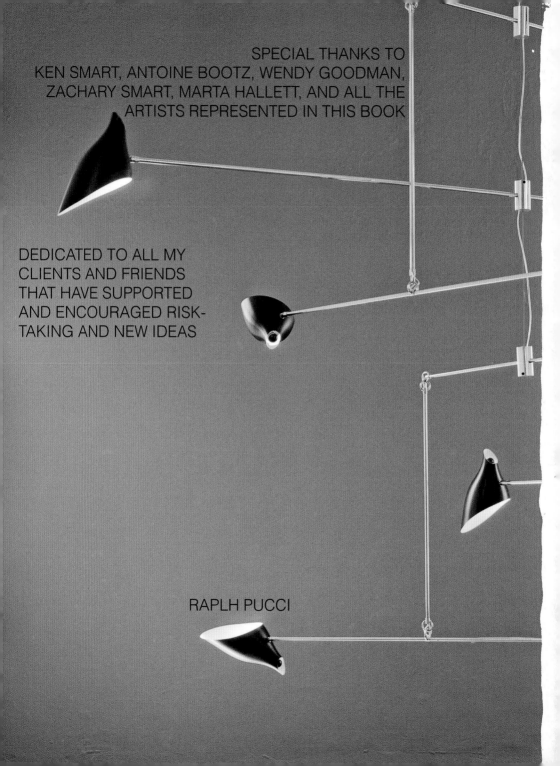

SPECIAL THANKS TO
KEN SMART, ANTOINE BOOTZ, WENDY GOODMAN,
ZACHARY SMART, MARTA HALLETT, AND ALL THE
ARTISTS REPRESENTED IN THIS BOOK

DEDICATED TO ALL MY
CLIENTS AND FRIENDS
THAT HAVE SUPPORTED
AND ENCOURAGED RISK-
TAKING AND NEW IDEAS

RAPLH PUCCI